Contents

Aztec Treasure Hunt

Graciela Vidal

SCHOLASTIC INC.
New York Toronto London Auckland Sydney
Mexico City New Delhi Hong Kong

Cover illustration and interior illustrations by Francis Back

3   4   5   6   7   8   9   10   23   10 09

1 The Hunt Is On

In 1914, a stranger arrived in the town of Kanab, Utah. His name was Freddy Crystal. He came to Utah after reading a newspaper story about some rock drawings. Crystal believed the rock drawings might put him on the trail of a lost, **ancient** treasure.

The news story led Crystal to Johnson Canyon, just north of Kanab. There, Crystal saw the rock drawings for himself. They seemed to point to nearby White Mountain. Crystal followed his hunch. He found hand-cut steps in the cliffs on White Mountain. The steps led to an opening in the mountain. But the opening was blocked. A large slab of rock had been used to seal it.

This discovery made Crystal wonder. Redrock was all around. But the slab was made of granite. Could this mean that the slab had been placed there to hide something? Crystal thought he had found the hiding place of the lost treasure.

Soon, everyone around Kanab heard of Crystal's discoveries. Groups of people rushed to White Mountain to join the search. They camped out in tents at the head of Johnson Canyon. They were willing to give up everything to find the hidden treasure. Everyone wanted to get a share.

The first job was to remove the granite slab. It took a lot of work, but Crystal and his volunteer crew finally did it. As they removed the stone from the opening, they saw a passage. But the passage was blocked by a second slab of granite. This slab was harder to remove than the first. But they kept at it.

When the treasure hunters finally removed the second block of granite, they were facing a tunnel. They explored 160 feet into the tunnel. Then they came to a **chamber**. From there, many tunnels led in different directions. Which way should they go?

The tunnels that led from the chamber were very dangerous. They could collapse and crush the explorers or trap them inside. Besides, people were tired of the long search.

The people of Kanab had left behind their farms, ranches, and stores to search for treasure. After two years, nothing had been found. People began to doubt that the treasure was there at all. They were ready to return to their lives. Soon life in Kanab was back to normal. The search for the hidden treasure had been all but forgotten.

Why did the treasure hunters give up?

Who Hid the Treasure?

Was Freddy Crystal right? Is there an ancient treasure hidden somewhere in the United States? If so, it might be worth millions in silver, gold, and emeralds. Some people believe it's out there. They believe it has been buried for almost five hundred years!

The treasure belonged to people who lived long ago. They were called Aztecs. The Aztecs lived in a rich and busy city in the Valley of Mexico. That is where Mexico City stands today. The Aztecs built beautiful palaces and temples there. They fought wars. They **conquered** other groups of people. Their empire grew bigger—and richer. It seemed like the Aztec empire could never fall.

Then one day, strangers arrived from a land far away. The strangers came in ships from across the ocean. They came from Spain. The Aztecs had to fight to protect their empire and try to save their treasure.

What became of the Aztecs? What became of their silver and gold? How could their treasure have ended up as far away as the United States? The treasure hunt begins with the story of the Aztec people.

Why do you think the Aztecs might have hidden their treasure?

3 People of the Sun

Nearly 1,000 years ago, the Aztecs lived in what is now Mexico. They were known as the "people of the sun." They believed that all life came from the sun. The Aztecs fought battles for the sun. They won many of these battles. They captured their enemies. They killed them to honor the sun god.

Many groups of people living in Mexico at that time did not like the Aztecs. They thought the Aztecs were too warlike. So, they joined forces and drove them away.

In the mid 1300s, the Aztecs came to the shores of a huge lake, Lake Texcoco. In the middle of the lake was a large rocky island. It was a difficult place to build and grow crops.

No other group had wanted to make a home there. But the Aztecs decided to make the island their home. On the island, they began to build a city. They called it Tenochtitlán.

Throughout the city, the Aztecs built a complex system of bridges and canals. Canoes carried supplies from the mainland and gifts from tribes the Aztecs had conquered.

In their city, the Aztecs also built large stone temples. The most important of them was the Great Temple. It stood nine stories high, in the center of the city. Here the Aztecs took the lives of people as offerings to the sun.

The Aztecs were proud of the Great Temple. Its walls were decorated with bright, colorful paintings. There were beautiful sculptures, too. The Great Temple showed the wealth and power of the Aztec people.

By the early 1500s, Tenochtitlán was a major city. Nearly 250,000 people lived and worked there. Wealthy **merchants**, artists, and other important people lived in fine houses of stone. Their yards were lined with colorful flowers. Everyone else lived in comfortable

huts, with roofs made of reeds and mud.

In the market square, thousands of people traded goods daily. Merchants sold jewelry, herbs, fabric, feathers, and animal skins. There was no such thing as money. Everything in the market was traded.

Outside the city, farmers raised crops. The Aztecs had developed an advanced system of farming. They dug canals around the fields where the crops were planted. The canals filled with rainwater. Then farmers scooped up thick mud from the bottom of the canals. They spread it on the soil in the fields. This rich muddy soil produced great crops of corn, beans, peppers, tomatoes, and squash.

The Aztecs believed in many gods. They asked their gods to help them in war, or to provide a good harvest. They believed that life would not be possible without the gods.

One of these gods was called Quetzalcóatl. His name means "feathered snake." The Aztecs believed he was fair-skinned and wore a beard. They told many stories about Quetzalcóatl. They said that he had sailed east on a raft of snakes. They believed that one day he would return to his kingdom. The Aztecs believed the time may have come.

What made them think so? Strange things had started to happen. A fiery shape had appeared in the sky. A temple had burst into flames. A weeping woman in the night had warned of danger. The Aztecs considered these signs that Qeutzalcóatl would soon return.

The Aztecs had a king named Moctezuma. But they believed that their empire really belonged to Quetzalcóatl. Moctezuma would give the empire back to the great god when he returned.

How would you describe the Aztec people?

4 Strangers Arrive

For nearly 200 years, the Aztecs built their empire. They conquered many other tribes. They ruled over several million people. They controlled all of what is now Mexico.

The Aztecs did not know that other lands lay beyond their empire. They did not know that across the ocean very different kinds of cities and people existed. But they would soon find out.

In 1492, the first European sailed across the Atlantic Ocean. His name was Christopher Columbus. He had convinced the queen of Spain to pay for his trip. In return, he promised her great riches. He was looking for a new trade **route** to India. Instead, he found land that the Europeans had not known about. It was North and South America. And Columbus called it the New World. He went back to Spain with tales of wonder and riches.

When Hernán Cortés, a Spanish explorer, heard such tales, he came to the New World to make his fortune. His first stops were in what are now the Dominican Republic and Cuba. From there, Cortés planned to sail across the Gulf of Mexico. He had heard of the great Aztec civilization and its great treasure.

Cortés arrived on the shores of the Aztec empire in April 1519. He had brought 550 men and 16 horses. Cortés set up a camp on the coast. He wanted to meet Moctezuma.

Moctezuma sent messengers to meet the strangers. The messengers brought many rich gifts. The treasures included a turquoise mask, a headdress of blue-green feathers, and bands of gold and jade to wear. The Aztecs thought that Cortés might be their god Quetzalcóatl. The messengers told Cortés that they had been sent by Moctezuma to pay respects. Cortés didn't correct their mistake. He told them that he, their god, was tired from his long journey.

Cortés had heard about the great riches of

the Aztecs. Now he could see for himself that the tales were true. Cortés figured the fortune was his for the taking.

The Aztecs had never seen anything like the Spaniards and their ships. Messengers told Moctezuma that the strangers came in great floating towers. They wore metal clothing from head to foot. Only their faces could be seen. But that wasn't all. They described how the strangers sat atop their enormous "deer." The Aztec people had never seen horses, either.

What terrified the messengers the most was the thing called a cannon. They said it was so loud, it made them deaf. A ball of stone flew out of its belly. And when it did, sparks shot out and it rained fire. The smoke had a bad smell, like rotten mud. When this thing was aimed at a tree, the tree split open.

But what really puzzled the Aztecs was the food the strangers ate. This thing called bread was large and white, but not heavy. It tasted a bit like corn flavored with honey. The Aztecs had nothing like it.

Moctezuma listened carefully. Was it possible that these strangers really were Quetzalcóatl and other gods? After all, they had come from the east. They had fair skin and beards. And they had come from a very different world.

Moctezuma sent his greatest warriors, his wisest men, and other important people to make a feast for the strangers. They worshipped the strangers like gods. But the strangers did not respect the Aztecs or their ways.

Moctezuma was shocked and frightened. Quetzalcóatl wasn't acting the way the Aztecs had expected him to. Had Moctezuma and his people done something wrong? Panic spread through the city.

Finally, word came that the strangers were coming to Tenochtitlán.

Why did the Aztecs think that Cortés and his men were gods?

5 Bad Guests

Hernán Cortés and his men couldn't wait to reach Tenochtitlán. They had gotten gifts of gold and **precious** stones. They were greedy for more. They also felt it was their duty to claim this new land for Spain. And they believed that the Aztec people should be taught to worship as they did.

Cortés made careful plans. Before leaving for the Aztec capital, he had his ships taken apart. He wanted to be sure that his men would not try to escape. Then Cortés gathered more soldiers for his army. He had no trouble finding native warriors willing to fight against the Aztecs. The Aztecs had conquered many people and made many enemies.

Finally, Cortés started toward Tenochtitlán. His soldiers killed thousands of people along the way. They even burned the temple to Quetzalcóatl and knocked down the statues.

When Moctezuma heard the news, he was baffled. Why would a god kill his own people and destroy his own temple? Who were these powerful strangers? What would be the best way to meet them? Moctezuma decided to greet them as friends. Moctezuma's chiefs thought he was wrong.

In November 1519, the Spaniards arrived in Tenochtitlán. Moctezuma was there to greet them. Many of his chiefs remained loyally by his side.

The Spaniards could not believe what they saw at Tenochtitlán. Cortés said it was the most beautiful city in the world. It was full of strange flowers and birds. People were everywhere. Canoes passed by in the lake and canals. The Spaniards were amazed.

Moctezuma tried his best to be a good host. He showed his guests around the city. He gave them parties with all kinds of foods. He let them stay in his father's ancient palace. But Moctezuma would soon figure out that the strangers had not come in peace.

As the days passed, the Spaniards began to guard Moctezuma more closely. They began to make rules. They said the Aztec gods were false. They said that the Aztecs must **convert** to Christianity. Finally, they demanded what they had really come for—treasure.

Cortés and his men took Moctezuma prisoner. Then they took all of the gold and silver, jade and turquoise, the crowns, the royal robes—everything. Then they melted the gold into coins.

In May 1520, Cortés took part of his army and left Tenochtitlán for the coast. He put a new commander in charge of the men he left behind.

Meanwhile, the Aztec people prepared for the Feast of Toxcatl at the Great Temple. It was the most important festival of the year. They played loud drums. They danced to celebrate.

On the day of the festival, the Spanish commander became worried. He thought the feast was getting out of control. He ordered his soldiers to attack. The Spaniards rushed to the

Great Temple. They began stabbing people with their swords. Anyone who tried to escape was injured or killed. Even those who ran indoors to hide were found and killed.

Aztec warriors hurried to the Great Temple to help their people. They fought the Spanish soldiers with stones and arrows. The Spaniards retreated back into the palace.

The Spaniards ordered Moctezuma to tell his people to stop fighting. Moctezuma went to the roof of the palace. He asked his people to give up the battle for the sake of the children. But the people attacked Moctezuma and called him a coward. Four days later, the Spaniards threw Moctezuma's body out of the palace.

Why do you think Moctezuma greeted the strangers as friends?

Trapping the Enemy

Moctezuma was dead. His people called him a **traitor.** They put his body on a pile of reeds. Then they set fire to it. Cuitláhuac became the new king of the Aztec people.

The Spaniards had been forced back into the palace, and now they were trapped there. The Aztecs surrounded the palace. They did not allow the Spaniards to have any food or fresh water. They blocked the canals. They closed off all the roads to the city. They waited for the Spaniards to starve to death.

The Spaniards could not survive without food and water. They decided to sneak out of the palace in the middle of the night. But they couldn't bear to leave the treasure behind. So

they took all the gold and jewelry they had found in the palace.

As quietly and quickly as they could, the Spaniards crossed the canals. They used a wooden bridge they had made. They had crossed three canals when an Aztec woman spotted them. They were caught! She began to shout that the Spaniards were escaping.

Aztec warriors rushed to stop the Spaniards. Some ran along the canals. Others paddled their boats at great speed. They surrounded the enemy. Then they attacked.

To escape, many Spaniards threw themselves into the water. But the gold and silver they were carrying was heavy. They sank and drowned. Hundreds of other Spaniards were either captured or killed.

The battle lasted all night. At dawn the Aztecs dragged the bodies out of the canals. Then they took back their treasure. They also took swords, steel helmets, shields, and armor from the dead soldiers.

The Aztecs celebrated their victory all summer long. They repaired the Great Temple. They cleaned up the city. They hoped that the Spaniards were gone for good.

Do you think the Aztecs have seen the last of the Spaniards? Why or why not?

7 End of the Empire

The Spaniards had suffered a great defeat. But, Cortés was not ready to give up the Aztec treasure. He and his men spent the next few months getting ready to return to Tenochtitlán. Cortés gathered a new army. He built new ships.

Back in Tenochtitlán, the Aztec people already were busy fighting a new enemy—smallpox. This disease spread quickly through the city. The native people of the New Word had never seen anything like it. The Spaniards had brought the germs with them from Europe. In Europe, smallpox had been around for a long time. People there had some **resistance** to the disease. But many native people died from it.

Their bodies didn't know how to fight these strange germs. Among the dead was Cuitláhuac. The Aztecs had lost two leaders.

In May 1521, the Aztecs learned that Cortés was returning to Tenochtitlán. This time the Spaniards came with trumpets, drums, and guns announcing their attack. Thousands of warriors from other tribes again joined the Spaniards to fight against the Aztecs.

Cortés had planned the attack well. His troops entered Tenochtitlán from the lake in every direction. The Spaniards pointed their cannons at the city. This time it was the Aztecs who were trapped.

The Aztec warriors fought bravely. But their canoes were no match for the Spanish ships. Their arrows were no match for the Spanish guns. People tried to escape from the city in canoes. Many left behind everything they owned.

The battle went on for eighty days. Soon there was no fresh water left in the city. There was no food. The people of Tenochtitlán could not go on. They were already weak from smallpox. The Aztecs lost to the Spaniards on August 13, 1521.

The Spaniards took young Aztec men for slaves. They set the city on fire. They tore down the buildings. The Great Temple was destroyed. When they were done burning and **looting**, the Aztec city was in ruins.

Over a quarter of a million Aztec people died during the battle. Many died from illness, polluted water, and lack of food. But the Aztecs were not the only victims.

By 1600, more than half the population of Mexico had died of smallpox and other European diseases. What was once the Aztec empire would now be ruled by the Spaniards. All the native people of Mexico were going to have to accept a new religion, a new language, and a new culture.

What happened to the native people who helped Cortés fight the Aztecs?

8

Hiding the Loot

So what happened to all the Aztecs' riches? Moctezuma had given the Spaniards some of his most precious gifts. And, as they destroyed Tenochtitlán, the Spaniards took all the gold, silver, and jewels they could find. They sent some of it back to the king of Spain. Cortés and his men kept some for themselves, of course.

But some people believe that the Spaniards did not take all of the Aztec treasure. Why? Stories say that the Aztecs took a great fortune out of Tenochtitlán. They say the Aztecs hid it from the Spaniards.

When the Spaniards first started stealing their gold and silver, the Aztecs must have gotten suspicious. They probably guessed that the Spaniards would try and take it all. They might have made plans to protect what they could.

No one knows for sure if there is any truth to the stories. No one knows if any Aztec treasure was hidden, and if so, where. Some people think it is hidden in one place. Others think it was hidden in many different places.

Some stories say that the Aztecs took their treasure north to what is now the United States. They may have been headed toward the ancient city of Aztlán. Aztlán was the place where the ancestors of the Aztecs had lived hundreds of years before—according to Aztec legend.

But no one really knows where Aztlán was located, or if it existed at all. Some people believe that the ancient city is now buried under lava at El Malpais, in New Mexico. Others say that Aztlán is somewhere in western Mexico. And still others believe that it might be as far north as Canada.

Some people believe that the ancient city

lies in Utah. Maybe they're right. The signs that Freddy Crystal found in Utah made people wonder. Did the Aztecs find the perfect hiding place in the mountains of Utah?

Do you think that Aztec treasure might still be hidden someplace? Why or why not?

9 Mystery in the Lake

In 1989, a man named Brandt Child returned to the Kanab area 75 years after Freddy Crystal's search failed. Child knew about the rock drawings that Crystal found. But he thought those signs were just a trick put there to throw treasure hunters off the track.

Child thought the treasure was hidden in a group of lakes six miles north of Kanab. He had found a drawing carved on the wall above the lake. It was a circle with an arrow pointing down. He believed this was an Aztec treasure sign.

A friend of Child's, Tony Thurber, dove to explore further. Right under the drawing, Thurber found a tunnel. It looked handmade.

It was four feet wide and seven feet high. Thurber entered the tunnel. He was about thirty feet into it, when something strange happened. A heavy flow of water poured through the tunnel. It tossed him around and around. He barely managed to leave the tunnel and return to the surface.

Thurber dove again. This time he went down with a line attached to his body. The line was held tightly by his helper. While he was underwater, Thurber felt the line go limp. He rushed back to the surface. Thurber asked his helper what had happened. Thurber was puzzled by what his helper said. His helper said that at his end, the line had been tight the whole time.

A few months later, Child's group went back to the site. This time, they had brought three professional divers with them. The divers went down. They measured the tunnel. It was 100 feet long. It ended in a room 80 feet wide.

It was late. The divers decided to quit for the day. That night, Russ, one of the divers, had a bad dream. He dreamed that he swam back

to the cave. In the dream, an Aztec warrior was waiting for him. The warrior was holding a spear. He threw the spear at Russ.

Russ was the first to dive the next morning. He was far into the tunnel when he felt someone grabbing and choking him. He began to scream. He was white as a sheet when the others helped him out of the water. Dream or no dream, what Russ had felt was real. Another diver went down. The same thing happened. He had to be pulled out when he felt someone choking him.

The divers left. They were scared. But it made the group want to search even more. They felt that there must be something down there. It was worth another try to find it. The divers came back two weeks later. Nothing had changed. As they explored the tunnel, the divers began to feel that they were choking. They had to be pulled up. This time the diving crew left for good. Once again, the search for the Aztec treasure had stopped.

To this day, no one has gone back to explore the tunnel in the lake. And no one has returned to White Mountain to continue the search Crystal started. As far as anyone knows, there may indeed be a great ancient treasure yet to be found. It might be in Utah—or maybe somewhere else.

If so, who will discover the legendary treasure of the Aztecs—the gold, silver, and emeralds hidden from the Spaniards? It could be anyone. It could be you!

Would you have given up the search or not? Why?

Glossary

ancient   very old, from another time

chamber   a large room

conquered   defeated and controlled by an enemy

convert   to change one thing into another

looting   massive public stealing, during a riot or a war

merchants   people who sell items for profit

precious   rare and valuable

resistance   the ability to fight back

route   the road or path used to get from one place to another

traitor   someone who helps the enemy; a person who betrays his or her country